Walk in Spirit

Prayers for the Seasons of Life

Lynn V. Andrews

ACACIA

PUBLISHING
CORPORATION

Published by Acacia Publishing Corporation
23852 Pacific Coast Highway, Suite 756
Malibu, CA 90265

Editor: Nancy Grimley Carleton
Cover Illustration: Angela C. Werneke
Cover Design: Lightbourne Images
Interior Illustrations: Andrea Massar
Book Design and Composition: Classic Typography

Manufactured in the United States of America.

10 9 8 7 6 5 4 3 2 1

Library of Congress Cataloging-in-Publication Data

Andrews, Lynn V.
    Walk in spirit : prayers for the seasons of life / Lynn
V. Andrews.
        p.   cm.
    ISBN 0–9650958–0–0 (hardcover)
    I. Prayers. I. Title.
BL560.A53   1996
291.4'3 — dc20   96–13039
                                                          CIP

For Agnes Whistling Elk and Ruby Plenty Chiefs,
Who taught me how to pray,
And for all those who pray
For peace and healing on Mother Earth.

*Acacia publishes books that inspire personal
growth and health in heart, mind, body, and spirit, and
raise people's consciousness to align with nature
and promote planetary healing and balance.*

Contents

Preface vii
Introduction to Shamanic Prayer 1

SPRING: PLANTING SEEDS 9

A Prayer for the Spring 12
Creating a Sacred Circle 13
Prayer for Death Arrow 17
Prayer for Life Arrow 18
Morning Light Prayer 19
Prayer for Strength 21
Prayer for Waking Up Power 24
For Birth and the Giving of Life 25
A Prayer for the Children 27

SUMMER: FULL BLOOM 29

A Prayer for the Summer 32
A Daily Affirmation of Power 34
Prayer of Joining Together 36
Prayer From the Heart 37
Invocation of the Fire Spirits 38
Entering the Silence 39
Prayer for the Afternoon Muses 41
A Prayer for Celebrating Puberty 43
A Prayer for Marriage and Partnership 47

FALL: GATHERING HARVEST 49

A Prayer for the Fall 52
Prayer for Truth 55
Wilderness Prayer at Eagle Point 58
Evening Sunset Prayer 62
I Am Full 65
A Prayer for My Mother and My Father 69
Prayer for Entering Menopause 71
A Prayer for Abundance 73

WINTER: TAKING STOCK 75

A Prayer for the Winter 78
Prayer in Times of Sadness 80
Prayer to Ask for Help 83
A Prayer for Balance 85
Masks of the Four Directions 87
Prayer for Healing 90
A Prayer for the Night 91
Prayer for the Wisdom of the Elders 93
A Prayer for Life and Death 95

GRATITUDE AND WORLD PEACE: OPENING THE HEART 99

A Prayer of Gratitude 103
A Thanksgiving Prayer 106
A Prayer of Thanks for the Animals 108
Morning Light Awakens 112
A Prayer for Peace 113

EPILOGUE: PRAYER CAN CHANGE THE WORLD 115

Preface

W*alk in Spirit* is a collection of prayers and thoughts inspired by the balance of nature and said with gratitude for the gifts of all creation. These prayers embody the heart and the soul of a person in search of higher consciousness. They are shamanic blessings. As a twentieth-century shaman, I live an everyday life of the Western world, but my teachers are native women from around the planet.

The prayers in this book help you to balance the incredible stress of our current life with the ecstasy of wisdom and understanding that have been part of so many native cultures throughout history. They include blessings for the seasons of the year, and for the seasons of the soul, the difficulties and joys that the soul encounters in life. In the late twentieth century, it can be difficult to live with a foot in spirit and a foot in the physical world. Oftentimes, the only bridge between these two worlds is prayer and contemplation.

These prayers are there for you when you need power. They will comfort you when you are in grief and help you sing in praise when you feel joy. They will inspire you if you already include the practice of prayer in your life, and they will teach you to pray, simply and experientially, if you have never learned.

In a world filled with by-rote endeavor, we so often perform the rituals of everyday life almost without thought. This is like driving down the freeway oblivious of the magnificent mountains and the diaphanous clouds above us. Because of our focus on our destination, we forget that life is a process and that this moment is all we will ever have. Sitting in the center of your own truth can bring you bliss and comfort. If you are not alive and aware and conscious now, you may never be. Prayer allows you to establish contact with the moment. It helps you travel the bridge between the physical world and the world of sacred vision. With prayer, you can change your life.

Without prayer, we may lose the world that we know forever. My teachers tell me that with prayer we can transform the negative state of our societies and bring Mother Earth back into balance. It is in this spirit that I offer the prayers in this book.

Lynn Andrews
Spring 1996

Introduction to
Shamanic Prayer

Shamanic prayer is different in many ways from the traditional forms of praying that so many of us have learned in the Western world. In shamanism, we pray to the Great Spirit, but we also pray to other aspects of power besides God or the Great Spirit. If we hold a ceremony for rain, for instance, we pray not only to the Great Spirit but also to Mother Earth and to the powers or guardians of the rain — approaching rain as if it is a being in itself. Rain is something that we consider as having life. It is an energy form, so prayer becomes an exchange of energy, a direct communication.

There are many great seers from the past, and in the present as well, who have expressed the power of shamanic prayer. Several of the women in the Sisterhood of the Shields, a group of forty four women shamans from around the world, have the ability, as an example of one of many, to call in the wind, to call in the rain and the thunder and lightning, to call in the spirits of being that influence weather.

I have heard that the Native American warrior Geronimo had great power with weather. He could call in the storms, and he could also ask them to leave. He did this by talking to the Spirit of the Wind. If you are a shaman, you have many allies — many guides and guardians and power animals — who can assist you in bringing in the power of the light forces in the universe.

This is sometimes confusing to people who have never understood the word *shamanism*. Shamanism, as I understand it, is having a sense of the oneness of the universe so that when you pray and ask for power or guidance from an element, say from a thunder being, you are praying to that thunder being, but you are also in that process understanding that within yourself, as a person of power, the thunder being makes up the oneness of the entire universe. So you are not only praying to the thunder being but are praying to the Great Spirit at the same time. One does not neglect the other, but in this particular case you are praying to an aspect of the Great Spirit that is represented by the manifestation of a thunder being.

Prayer, as my teachers and I practice it, always entails an opening of the heart. Prayer arises from a sense of gratitude for all that is — for the magnificence and the miracle of life. So prayer can be sitting on top of a mountain, sitting in a sacred circle somewhere in the wilderness, or sitting in your home silently in a state of introspection and serenity and simply experiencing the bliss and the power of the universe in harmony all around you.

I have dedicated my life to this work, to shamanism, the balancing of the energies of the world around me. I know that the earth will heal herself if given the chance, that our magnificent bodies are a miracle and will heal themselves if given the chance. It is only ignorance, in my way of thinking, that creates the misery and the pain in this world. It is out of ignorance that we cut down the rain forests so that oxygen levels and the ozone are disturbed and possibly destroyed. We wouldn't do such things unless we lacked the awareness to understand the wholeness of life.

We are all energy forms on a giant matrix of energy lines that run throughout the world, throughout the universe. If I make a prayer in California, it affects the other ends of those energy vectors somewhere around the earth. I believe that in prayer we can make a difference on this planet. I believe that Mother Earth can be healed. I believe that we can change. I believe in the goodness of life, and the goodness inherent in each and every one of us. But we need consciousness. We need awareness. We need to reach across cultural boundaries everywhere in the world with our hands open and receptive to the dignity and the integrity of all cultures in all ways of thought that support the light.

Prayer is an openness of heart, a settling into the center of your being. You can pray with words, with song, with ceremony, with an altar, in a shrine, in a temple, in a church, at the side of a pond, in the heart of nature sitting in the center of a power spot—it doesn't matter, because *you* are the prayer. It is your essence and life force that bring down the power of the universe into your body, because you are an antenna calling in the forces of light and joy and healing. The powers of Father Sky come down into your body to meet the forces of Mother Earth. The nature beings, powers of the elements, and the four directions come up through you and meet in your power center. If you are trained and skilled, you can receive that energy and power and create more light, more strength, and more harmony in the world.

Praying With Your Children and Loved Ones

People often ask me how to share prayer with children and family. From my point of view, your whole life is a prayer. But there are certainly times for engaging in a more focused and conscious form of prayer. I encourage people to pray once a day with their children and with the people they love. The easiest way is to pick up a book of prayers, such as this one, and simply sit, holding hands or not, and read a selection from the book. Read a prayer that is inspiring, because when you are inspired by words that are beautiful, something inside of you changes and is enhanced. Your heart opens, and when your heart expands and allows the life force to enter, then you are establishing a relationship with the Great Spirit and the powers of the life force that surround you.

To gain a child's attention, creating a ceremony helps. Ask your child to gather four stones, or eight, or twelve, to create a sacred circle. Have your child place them together with you in a circle; then sit within the circle, and create a prayer together that touches on the most important things in your life at that time. Create a ceremony with your child in celebration of small things as well as big things. Pray to celebrate a good grade or to acknowledge any obstacle your child has overcome.

We have so few rituals and ceremonies in our lives today. We seldom celebrate the major rites of passage, such as the development of a young girl or boy into puberty. We need to celebrate a daughter's first blood or a boy's coming into maturity with a rite of passage. It is crucial to mark your child's passage from one season of growth to another. Prayer is an integral part of this process. Just as it is important to celebrate the changing seasons of a year, so is it important to celebrate the seasons of one's life — birth, puberty, marriage, menopause, death. Prayers for the seasons of your soul help you to grow.

How to Use This Book

One useful and comfortable way to approach this book is to flip through it and select a prayer. Or you might look at the table of contents and select a prayer that speaks to you about a particular concern you are having. Another approach is to follow the seasons of the year by using the prayers related to that season. It is interesting to consider the symbology, to think of seasons of the soul as they correspond to seasons of the year. Perhaps you will find a rhythm within your own being that relates to the paradigm that is set out in this book.

These prayers are for you. They are only suggestions, something that perhaps may inspire you to

write your own prayers—to see that the act of praying is not really difficult. So use this book as you
see fit, always remembering that the Great Spirit is
ever with you, supporting your efforts to become a
prayerful person. Move forth, warrior spirit, discover
the teachings of this lifetime, and act upon them.
Pray upon them. Truly find what you have come here
to learn.

Spring

Planting Seeds

Spring is akin to the beginning cycle of life. Spring is when the seeds are planted. During wintertime, you hibernate and hold close to you all that you have accomplished during the year, and you discard what no longer serves you, so that in the spring, in the first planting of the year, you have a sense of what it is that you need to accomplish in the months ahead. As a warrior of spirit, you need to choose your target. You need to define that target and understand what is needed to take you toward your goals.

Planting seeds requires great care. You must first till the soil and choose the fertilizer carefully. Symbolically, this includes the education of your body so that you are ready for what is next, so that you are physically capable of carrying out what is needed for the planting. Then you gather your seeds, or bring forth the seeds you have saved throughout the past years, and you choose the seeds that are important. In a sense, this is like an archer making sure that the bow is well aimed. You are gathering energy. When you plant a seed, you are planting and cultivating energy so that the life force will find its way toward the light and blossom and become a manifested reality. A plant will then grow into full bloom as the seasons turn. You are gathering your forces so that when the planting happens in the springtime, life will surely follow.

Spring is the time of the life/death prayer arrows. You place all that you want to give away to the universe into the death arrow, and you burn it symbolically, either in visualization or in an actual ceremony. Then you place all of your acts of power, the ten things that you are going to do in the coming year to make your act of power a reality, into the life arrow. Then you give the arrow away to the universe. This practice sets you on your course for the rest of the year.

May spirit and love surround you in your journey through springtime. May your spirit awaken, and may your seeds grow and bear fruit.

A Prayer for the Spring

Great Spirit, as you empower the flowers
To the brightness of spring color,
I honor my long winter of introspection
And bring forth my new beginnings.
Mother Earth, I plant my love, my seeds,
From the sacred gourd of plenty
Into your gracious land.
I listen for the language of the drums,
The symbols of the sacred shields, to enlighten me.
I pull back the bow of my being
In expectation of my new acts of power.
I set the arrow of my intent,
As my spirit begins to grow.
Thank you for honoring my sacred garden
And the seeds that I have imparted to you
With my trust and innocence.
May I hear the winds of communication from you,
Great Spirit, as I walk this great Mother Earth
As she awakens in beauty. Ho!

Creating a Sacred Circle

I call the sacred powers of all directions
To be with me now.
I banish any energies that wish me ill will.
I call the power of Mother Earth, the Great Turtle,
Slow one, necessary one,
The one who carries us on her shoulders,
The earth spirit who teaches us patience,
Who teaches us to take one step at a time,
Powers of the Earth, come in!

Powers of the South, Sacred Mouse,
Come into the center of my circle.
Sacred Mouse, teacher of trust and innocence,
Teach me to see what is right in front of me,
So that I may gather learning, gather trust,
Gather the power of touching others
In gentle, healing ways.
Power of the South, the Mouse, come in!

Powers of the West,
Place of intuition, of looking within,
Woman place inside all of us,
Home of the Great Bear,
Come into my circle here and now.
Bear, with your sacred task of hibernation,
Of dreaming, come into my circle.
Teach me to go inside and listen.
Teach me to go inside all the winter of my life,
Into the darkness, without fear, with excitement,
With your great power, Sacred Bear.
I pray that I will learn to be quiet,
To hear my inner voice, to distinguish
The voice of my intuition from the false voices
Of fear, doubt, and indecision.
Powers of the West, sacred intuition, Sacred Bear,
Come into my circle now!

Powers of the North, place of storms of wisdom,
Mountains of knowledge,
Come in, Buffalo, to my circle, now!
Teach me how to give away,

To share what I have learned,
To nourish others with the bounty of my being.
Teach me to face the cold,
To stand alone when I must,
To take care of others like a tribe, like a true circle.
Buffalo, sacred provider,
Provide me with wisdom, with knowledge,
And with the ability to share what I learn.
Powers of the North, come into my circle, now!

Powers of the East, come into my circle.
Be in the middle of my life, now.
Teach me how to rise above my daily vision,
My tired eyes, into new vistas of sight.
Teach me to take my vision to my higher self.
Teach me to let the vision of my higher self down
Into my daily mind to revitalize my life.
Teach me to prey upon
Whatever does not feed my higher purpose,
And to rid myself of false paths that do not serve me.
Great bird of spirit, Sacred Eagle,
Powers of the East, come into my circle now!

Powers of the Sky, Great Spirit,
Fill my circle now with your great light,
As I envision my circle surrounded
By infinitely bright yellow light.
I am enveloped in your great glow,
Touched deep inside by your power of healing.
I stand here in the center of my being and call
My brothers and sisters to the center of their being.

May the Great Spirit, the one who carries us,
Nourish our circle and
Allow the powers of the earth—
The south, west, north, and east—
To shine in and through us,
Enlightening our circle and teaching us
Peace, joy, and wisdom.
May all the powers of all directions
Guide us and keep us. Ho!

Prayer for Death Arrow

Great Spirit, Mother Earth,
Powers of the four directions,
My power animal, my allies, my ancestors,
And all who love me, hear me now.
This is a prayer for my act of power.
Thank you for being with me.
I honor your presence within my circle,
My sacred circle.
This is my death prayer arrow.
These are all the things that have kept me
From my act of power all this long time.
These are the things I am willing to give away, *
So that I may accomplish my act of power,
My act of destiny, in this lifetime.
With this next year, I will begin. Ho!

*Here you may list all of what you are willing to give away, but only make the declaration if you know you can accomplish it.

Prayer for Life Arrow

Great Spirit, Mother Earth,
Powers of the four directions,
My power animal, my allies, my ancestors,
And all who love me, hear me now.
This is a prayer for my act of power.
Thank you for being with me.
I honor your presence
Within my circle,
My sacred circle.
This is my life prayer arrow.
*There are things that I will do,** *
So that I may accomplish
My act of power,
My act of destiny, in this lifetime.
With this next year, I will begin. Ho!

*Here you may list all that you are going to achieve.

Morning Light Prayer

I would like to offer a prayer
To the morning light,
To the morning light that shimmers
On the face of the lakes,
And reflects the shadows of the great mountains
Across the faces of stone.
To the morning light that traces
The outline of the beloved,
And finds the field mouse
Scampering in the meadows.

It is in the morning light
That baby horses experience
Their first mouthfuls of sweet green grass.
It is in the morning light
That I walk beneath the trees,
And hear the wind singing from the north,
Bringing me messages
From the Great Spirit.

I watch the hawks high in flight.
I ask them to take a prayer to the Great Mother,
And tell her of my love for her.

Morning light from the great sun,
Our father power,
Fill me with warmth and strength for my day.
Illumine my path,
That I may understand where I am going.

Morning light,
The shadows of darkness
Flee from your awesome glow.
Morning light, you are like a child
I would hold and cherish.

Oh Great Spirit,
Thank you for your mysterious ways,
And help me to walk in your light
Forevermore. Ho!

Prayer for Strength

Great Mother Goddess,
Sower of dreams,
On this fecund Mother Earth,
Help me to experience your light
In every moment of my life.
Help me to experience your dream
In my earth walk.
As a beautiful rose growing in my being,
Let me breathe in
The perfume of your essence
And your perfection,
Permeating every cell in my body.

You have given me blood, Great Mother,
Blood, the carrier of my future incarnations.
Help me to serve you well,
So that I may know my lifetimes
As they have imprinted my spirit shield
With the image of your face.

You are the power
That motivates me,
That brings me closer
To my shaman center,
And to my psychic equilibrium.
You are the one
Who fills me with inspiration,
Who helps me to feel the rose within—
The perfection of physicality
And spirit manifested
In my earth walk.
You are a wrathful
And a benevolent ruler.
Help me not to fear
The shadow side of myself,
The dark side of my femininity.
I am Crazy Woman,
And I am the Rainbow Mother.
I am Death Mother,
And I am the Great Nurturing Mother.
The sacred cross of feminine power
Lives within me.

As I see your sacred face
Reflected in the eyes
Of my sisters and brothers,
Great Mother Goddess,
Give me the strength
To follow your path,
To feel your rose within me,
To plant my seeds on this earth,
And reap the wisdom as they grow.
Help me to change and to be strong
Throughout the coming year.
Great Mother,
I honor you
All the days of my life. Ho!

Prayer for Waking Up Power

I am a shaman.
I am a false face magician.
I come from the faraway.
I am a person of words.
With this face, I will heal.
With this new face,
I will bring joy into the world.
I am a person of words.
I am a shaman.
I am spirit.
I come from the faraway.
I bring waves to the water
And wind to the trees.
I heal the mind and the heart.
With this face, I see you.
With these new eyes, I see you.
I am four eyes now,
For I have my new shaman face. Ho!

For Birth and the Giving of Life

Great Spirit, you have brought me new life.
Celebration is upon us
And all the spirits and souls among us.
A new child is born!

The beauty of your face,
Your tiny hands!
Your voice is heard throughout
The eons of time,
For you have been here before,
Small one.
The radiance of the Great Spirit
Shines through your eyes.
I see the ages in your vision.
I welcome your beautiful
Being into my world.
Let me know, little one,
For I am your mother.

I am here for you.
Let me brighten your way
And soften your pain.
May you learn what you have
Come here to learn.

You are free, my child,
For I do not own you.
You stand in freedom as do I—
Both of us great trees in the same forest.
We share the same ground.
We share the shade of our leaves
And our love of the sky.
Though I love you with my whole being,
I choose not to make your will my own,
For life is yours to choose
Forevermore.

Thank you, Great Spirit,
For the blessings and the miracle of life. Ho!

A Prayer for the Children

As I look across the great expanse
Of wilderness,
I think of what is important and sacred in this life,
And I think of the children.
We are in a life where we must protect the children.
The children are sacred.
The children, beyond all others,
Must be recognized and honored
For their presence.
The hope of the world is with them.

It is our responsibility
To tear away the veils of ignorance
For our children, so that they may learn
What is real and what is true.
A wilderness untouched by human hands is
Like the map of spirit within a child.
It is open to experience, to the newness of life.
Let spirit imprint the souls of the children

With light and radiance.

It is we adults who change the face of growth
In our children.
We are the ones who
Destroy the vision of the young.
We take our will and ask our children to live
In our shadow.
We want our will to be theirs.
Great Spirit, help adults to understand the children.
Let there be no harm.
Great Spirit, carve a trail for the young ones,
So that they may grow strong and free
And full of light.
Thank you, Great Spirit, for hearing my words.
I ask you for the children
Who do not yet know how to pray.
Help them to see your face and hear your words
Forevermore. Ho!

Summer

Full Bloom

Summer is the season of full bloom. All the seeds that you have planted into our Earth Mother will show themselves to you now. Summer brings the magnificence of all that you have conceived and planted, presenting itself to the world. Your colors are bright in summer. They are presented with a depth of appreciation, beauty, and gracefulness for the accomplishment that is there. Summer is filled with appreciation for what you have done, for your accomplishment, for your growth, and for your strength to move toward the spiritual light of creation, the celebration for the harmonies and the balance that exist in all of life.

Summer is a time of mirrors. To see your own reflection within your symbolic creations takes stillness and action at the same time. As you nourish your planting with movement, you still the storm of mind chatter and emotional confusion in your heart and settle the wind inside you. Only a gentle breeze of spirit is needed to turn the flowering toward you so the mirrors can be seen.

These mirrors celebrate your reflection and teach you what is needed to complete the cycle of seasons in the fall and winter. The summer solstice is a ritual of flowering and pruning. The end of summer is the fulcrum balance point for the seasonal year.

For the warrior of spirit, summer is a time to shoot your arrow toward the target you have chosen, and let the arrow take flight. It is a time of power.

During the summer, may you gather your forces for the reaping of what you have created. May you manifest the sacred weaving of your life into reality. May you celebrate all the beauty and vibrant color that you are.

A Prayer for the Summer

Great Mother, as we see you
At the heart of our world,
We give thanks to you for our life force,
And the gifts of our physical being.
With this gift of life,
You have presented us with the mirrors of existence
That elevate our soul toward the highest light.
Every day we are faced with these reflections,
And they bring us great pain and great joy.
In our pain, we forget we are on a great journey.
We struggle within the confines of our ignorance,
Desperately searching for a way
To tear away the veils that cloud our vision.
Great Mother, help us on our journey of discovery.
Give us power to continue to seek.
Help us to find joy and courage,
As we navigate through the dense fog of confusion.
Help us, Great Mother, to understand your needs,
And what it takes to heal your precious body.

In our commitment to you,
We make a commitment to ourselves,
To our own enlightenment,
To our own process of forgiveness and wisdom.
In this forgiveness, I make a pledge from my heart,
To find an end to this weakness and pain,
To find a harmony and a balance,
So that we may more successfully walk
With a foot in the physical and a foot in spirit.
Oh Great Mother, I humble myself to your power.
At this moment, I visualize golden white light
Surrounding me and enabling me to move
Into my shaman center, into my place of power,
A perfect reflection of your innocence.
I see the shield that you carry
Shining like a beacon in the darkness.
Your shield is made of trust and faith:
Trust that each and every one of us will build
A rainbow bridge across the abyss of darkness.
Faith symbolized by each of us crossing that bridge,
Held forever in your light.
Great Mother, we give thanks for your blessings. Ho!

A Daily Affirmation
of Power

I am a new warrior of spirit.
I exist in a world of sacred balance.
I balance with one foot in the physical world
Of material substance and
One foot in the dimensions of spirit and sacred life.
My course is set by my ally, the winds of time.
Mother Earth gives me life force,
The life blood of my sacred body.
The plants give me nourishment and healing,
As I ride the windhorse of my intent—
My sacred warrior's transport of buoyant joy—
Into a new and unknown world of harmony.

I am truly a new warrior,
An androgynous spirit being of light,
Like the angels who surround me.
My weapons are the shields of awareness,
The symbols of ancient trust and the sacred give-away.

I share my heart with those who need me,
But few see me for who I really am.
I do commerce in the world.
I raise my family.
I live a life dedicated to freedom.
I immerse myself in the physical world
So that one day I can give it up,
Because I can only give up what I truly have.
People learn from me through example,
Because of the integrity of my own life and spirit.
I move into the world with confidence and wisdom.
I am open and innocent.
I am always learning tools of knowledge,
And I share these tools with my sisters and brothers.

I am a warrior of the light,
And I live the integrity of that truth with great care
From a center within myself that is pure goodness,
The embodiment of the peaceful soul.
I walk with confidence
The path of heart and personal power. Ho!

Prayer of Joining Together

We are all a circle.
Our dreams and prayers are at their core
The same dreams and prayers.
Our circle will lead out into the world,
And spread harmony over all the earth.
To remind us of this circle,
We envision one knot.
This knot will bind us together
In higher circles,
Each of us responsible for
One other person's prayer,
Responsible for each other's prayers,
And the prayer that our circle represents.
We offer our knots up to the Great Spirit.
We are now separate,
And we are now joined.
May our prayers be as one.
May our unique spirits thrive
Independently and together. Ho!

Prayer From the Heart

Great Spirit, whose voice we hear
In the winds and the trees,
Mother Earth, whose breath gives us life:
Help us to walk in beauty and strength,
And to learn the lessons that are hidden
In the stones and the trees
And the waters of the sea.
Give us the strength to fight
Our greatest enemy — ignorance.

Great Spirit, hear the sounds
Of our grateful hearts,
And help us to find
The wisdom and joy and power
That is locked within each of our souls.

We are the reflections of you, Great Spirit,
Join us on our path as we join you,
For all the days of our lives. Ho!

Invocation of the Fire Spirits

Spirit of the winged ones,
Great Eagle Mother,
Fly into my body,
Fly into the bodies of us all,
And bring to me,
Bring to us all,
The flaming power of the sun.

Power of the salamanders,
Awaken now!
Quicken my blood.
Quicken the blood of us all.

Power of the sun,
Carrier of my star shield,
Power of the inner fire,
Arousal of the inner flame,
Center within our spirits,
Now! Ho!

Entering the Silence

Great Spirit, let the guardians
Of our dreams
Stand as sentinels around our beings
As we move into the silence,
As we move into that place of stillness
And quietude where spirit dwells.
Listen to the winds
As they come out of the four directions.
Name the winds that are your allies.
Listen to the birds and the language of nature
And the breath of summer.
You are each reflections of the Great Spirit.
The Great Spirit blesses you and comes
When you are most silent.
Let your silence be like a prayer in the night,
Soft and quiet, full of integrity.
Let your bliss move up
Through your body from Mother Earth,
Up into your heart, opening your heart chakra,

Making you vulnerable to something new and radiant
That wishes to become a part of you.
The first lesson of power is that we are alone.
The last lesson of power is that we are all one.
Great Spirit, there is an enormous chasm
Between those two statements.
Most of us spend lifetimes bridging that gap.
Silence of the mind, silence within the spirit,
Is a great bridge for that movement
Between body and spirit and aloneness,
And loneliness and aloneness.
Great Spirit, let us feel your hand on our backs.
May the wind caress us as the breath of your spirit
As we move into the sacred silence,
So that we can hear your words.
Thank you, Mother Earth.
Thank you, Great Spirit.
Thank you, my ancestors,
The four-leggeds and the winged ones,
And all the sacred beings that surround me.
Thank you for being with us now. Ho!

Prayer for the Afternoon Muses

So often in the afternoon,
I become restless, Great Spirit.
So I have learned, thanks to your wisdom,
Great Spirit, to create in the afternoon.
I have learned that the afternoon
Is the perfect time to learn something new,
So I thank you for this most sacred of times.
When the sun becomes lower in the sky,
I begin to paint.
I sit with a pad and a pen,
And I begin to write.
I feel the muses
Waking up from their slumber
As they look over my shoulder,
Fascinated to see what I am creating.

Inspiration so often does not visit you,
Unless you are performing your art.

If you wish to create a work of art,
Begin to paint,
And the inspiration will come.
If you wish to write something inspiring,
Sit down and begin,
And the muses will come.
They will join you in your effort
And lend you strength and ideas.
It is the spirit of the afternoon
That comes close and comforts you.
It wants you, this afternoon being,
To be at ease.
Turn the phone off.
Drink something that pleases you.
Find yourself a special natural setting
Where the little people can join you,
And the etheric beings of the trees can
Lend you their sparkle.
Afternoon is a time of gathering and expression.
It is a good time to pray. Ho!

A Prayer for
Celebrating Puberty

*Great Mother, when a child begins
On the trail toward adulthood,
Prayers are needed.
Reaching the great gateway of puberty, dear child,
Your universe is like a wilderness.
You look across the vast expanse of your life to come,
And you see only uncharted territory,
Full of challenges and excitement.
You are becoming, like a seed that has been planted
Into rich earth, beginning to grow.
You are fecund with all possibilities.
You will blossom soon,
Your branches reaching up toward the sky.
You cannot imagine the days not being long
And full of joy.
The pains of older people are hard to understand
When you are so busy trying to comprehend
The changes in your own body.*

Great Mother, lend your wisdom
To the path of all young people.
Help them be strong.
Help them to relax into the changes
In moods, knowing always that it is you
Who are helping them to grow
And to become full in this life.
You have begun the process of preparing their bodies.
Help them to understand your grace.
Help them to grow straight and strong,
Like giant trees,
Pure in purpose and singular on their path
Toward your likeness and your radiance.

Thank you, Great Mother,
For watching over this rite of passage.
All those who reach this age,
May you be clear of purpose,
Remembering that yours is a path of heart,
And when troubles are upon you,
Do not forget Mother Earth
And how she supports you and gives you life.

Remember to heal her and to let her wisdom be yours.
Walk your path knowing that the Great Mother
Has her hand on your back, giving you
Encouragement and blessings every step of the way.

If you are a woman, a young girl, a first blood,
Look across the sacred wheel,
And directly opposite you will find the
Position of wise blood.
At first blood, you look toward
The challenges of motherhood one day soon.
But to balance that progression in time,
Look toward wise blood,
The gateway to higher spiritual life,
Knowing that now is the time
To accomplish, to understand the physical realm.
Your body is asking you to do this.
So give blessings toward your body
And the changes that are happening.

For a boy reaching puberty, he, too,
Is looking toward parenthood, union,

And making acts of power in the world,
Just as the young girl is.
It is at this point in your life that
Accomplishment is important.
You are building the foundation for your spirit lodge,
The lodge of your spirit in physical totality.
As a boy, you look across the sacred wheel,
And you also see the gateway to higher spirit life
Directly across from you.

Know the positions on the sacred wheel, young ones.
Know that this is your time of physicality,
Your time to get your act together,
So that when the great gateway of spirit
Is upon you in mid-life, you will be ready.
You will have done the building of
Your sacred foundations.
The Great Mother wishes you great courage and
Will be praying for you all the days of your life. Ho!

A Prayer for Marriage and Partnership

As I cross the desert in the evening time,
I look ahead at twin peaks,
Two magnificent mountains
Rising up out of the desert floor,
Reflecting the setting sun with purples
And oranges and magenta.
These mountains, so similar in stature,
Yet standing apart from one another,
Are married in the earth,
The roots of their being intermingling,
Taking life force and extending that energy
To the sky fathers and the great cloud beings
That circulate above them.
Great Spirit, a marriage is a beautiful moment.
But how many times have I seen a great woman,
Her spirit shield shining in the morning light,
Meet a magnificent man,
Who holds his spirit shield high, reflecting the sun.
At the moment of marriage, however, the man's

Shield is placed on top of the woman's shield,
And her designs are hidden and scattered
To the four winds.
She is lost into the identity of his shield forever.
What is to become of her spirit?
Great Spirit, I pray for all marriages and partnerships.
I pray that they honor
Each person's identity and individuality,
Like twin peaks,
Shining now in the setting sun,
Each reflecting different shadows,
Different moments of light and darkness,
But each grounded together forever
In sacred Mother Earth.
I pray, Great Spirit, that all marriages
Bring a kinship of souls and a kindling of freedom.
Hold your hands and arms open,
You who are about to marry,
Allowing the winds of heaven to blow between you,
Fire and earth, water and sky, commingling,
But always retaining the individuality
And the presence of sacred being. Ho!

Fall

Gathering Harvest

*F*all is a season of reckoning, a time when all that you have sown and all that has blossomed is now to be reaped. It is a time of gathering, a time of great beauty, and a time of change and letting go. So often we are terrified of change, not only because of the mystery of the unknown but because change implies letting go of what we do know and what we have always held as a kind of security in our lives. Even bad habits can provide a kind of security.

So fall is a time to pray for understanding and for the strength to reap what serves you and to discard what holds you back from your enlightenment and your true power in the world. You have chosen your arrow in spring. You have pulled back the bow, you have set the arrow, and you have even chosen the target. In summer, the time when your arrow makes its flight and reaches its mark, you blossomed. In fall you are in a time of reckoning.

In some of the ancient languages of the world, the

word *sin*, when translated, means "missing the mark." It signifies losing the opportunity you had, because once you sow the seed, and once that seed blossoms, you must then reap what you deserve, what is yours. In the fall, you are pulling in all of your energies and thoughts that have been scattered outward throughout the year. Collect them in, like sheep gathering back to the fold. Then let go of what is no longer essential to your life process, whatever misses the mark.

During the fall, may you find the strength to be all that you are. May you reap all the abundance of the universe that is meant for you.

A Prayer for the Fall

Great Spirit, Mother Earth,
Powers of the four directions,
My allies, my medicine animal, my ancestors,
And those who love me,
Be here with me now, and hear my prayer.

Beyond the landscapes of ordinary life
Lie dimensions of higher consciousness
And perfected reality.
Somewhere in your dimension, oh Great Spirit,
The Great Mother opens her arms
And receives our spirit shields,
Which spin for all eternity.
This earthly life is a gift from you, Great Mother.
I honor your presence in my life, Great Spirit,
And your gift of eternal life.
I know that my spirit shield is in need of balancing,
That in this lifetime I have the opportunity
To tear away the veils of ignorance

And walk the earth in my sacred androgynous form,
Balanced equally between
The male and female energies,
Within myself and within the cosmos.

I will manifest within this lifetime my true destiny
By finding the hidden passions
That live within my heart and my soul,
Those hidden passions for truth,
For harmony and balance and goodness,
That live within me.
I will not be afraid to look at
The dark side of my being.
That dark side is my instinctual nature,
Which I have denied in some way in my life.
To repress who I really am is to live a lie,
And to live my life through the eyes of others,
Not through my own eyes.
I pledge, Great Mother, to take responsibility
For who I am in this life,
For my weaknesses and my strengths.
I pledge to walk the path

As a spiritual warrior of heart.

As I see the many mirrors I have created
Around me in my life,
I will not be afraid to look in them.
And I will realize that no matter what reflection I see,
It is the reflection of some aspect of you, Great Spirit,
And for that I will love all that I see.

To take my power in this lifetime
Is to understand that I am made of power, and
That power is the reflection of you, Great Spirit.
I understand that the first lesson of power is
That we are alone in the struggle
Toward enlightenment.
I also understand that the last lesson of power is
That we are indeed all one.
You are my light and my love and my way,
Oh Great Spirit,
And I honor you all the days of my life. Ho!

Prayer for Truth

Great Spirit,
I honor you all the waking days of my life.
Oh great wise ones
Who guide us on our sacred journey,
You know when to reveal the mysteries of truth,
Just as the clouds part
And allow us to see the snowcapped mountains
That were obscured from view.
I am learning that truth burns like a fire,
And when I am filled with psychic debris
That I have collected in my experiences
Through my lifetime,
Truth, at the wrong moment,
Can burn me beyond recognition.
Thank you, Great Spirit,
For helping me understand
That my journey is a careful one
And that I must place each foot
Carefully on the path,

Walking with judgment and discernment.
It is inappropriate to run wildly and carelessly
On this sacred journey.
Even with this knowledge,
I am grateful for my spontaneity,
And my wildness of spirit.
I understand the difference
Between the wildness of my own soul
And carelessness and thoughtlessness
On my path to evolution.

As I look out at my sacred landscape,
I see great boulders that look like eagles,
And clouds that look like wolves,
Passing above me in the sky.
The great thunderhead clouds
Reflect kachina dolls dancing
In the spirit world across the sacred plains.
The mountains rise majestically above the clouds,
And the rivers flow like luminous fibers of silver
Through the life force of my universe.
I hold hands with my sisters and my brothers,

Committed to harmony and peace,
And an understanding of the human condition.
Truth has many names, but all truth is the same.
Those who say that they know the truth
Know nothing.
And those who say that they know nothing
Know the truth.
Thank you, Great Spirit,
For this magnificent schoolhouse we call earth.
Thank you, Great Spirit,
For the winged ones and the four-leggeds
And the two-leggeds.
Thank you for the plants and
The trees and the stones
That were here before us and that teach us
So many things.
I give you my trust, Great Spirit,
As you have given me my life.
Thank you for your blessings. Ho!

Wilderness Prayer
at Eagle Point

Great Spirit, thank you
For letting me see the beauty of your face.
I see your being in the reflected sunlight
Of your still, northern waters.
I see your passion in the froth
Of your waves at sunset,
As the seals look toward us with curiosity and care.
I remember my own feelings of trepidation and awe,
As I see your magnificence in the
Untouched wilderness of this great Mother Earth.
When I see the logs floating on the surface
Of your satiny sea,
I wonder what they felt when they, entire tribes,
Were cut and flung away down the slopes,
Into northern inlets of your body.
I honor you, the majesty of you,
The flight of your birds,
The long slender legs of the blue herons,

Perched on a dock far to the north.
I watch the reflection of the fall sun
In the eyes of those herons,
And I see the turning of the seasons,
Just as those seasons are felt in my own body
And my own spirit.
I know that nothing is forever,
That we own nothing,
Not even the ideas that we express as truth.
They are your ideas; they are not ours.
Yet I thank you for the instrument that
Gives me the strength to express these truths.
I watch the purity of being,
The stillness of the waters,
The blue of the sky, and then the setting sun.
I wonder at creation and the meaning of it all.
I wonder if I will ever truly understand
Why I am here
And how your bliss fills my heart and why.

I thank you for the opportunity
To feel you inside me,

As I see you inside the universe,
Expressing pure light, pure joy,
Into our presence.
I am yours, Great Spirit,
As I have been a hollow log with your essence
Flowing through me.
I am the bamboo with your life force
Expressing itself through every particle
And every branch.
Now I am the seeing that recognizes you
And honors you
And asks you to teach me more.
Let me be of service to you all my waking days.
Let me be the representative of the
Great Goddess Mother in all of her aspects—
I am mother, I am daughter, I am lover,
And I am goddess sacred woman
With every breath that I take.

When I look at your northern waters,
I am reminded of coming winter,
Of the coldness and the wind

And the glaciers moving slowly,
Like my own sense of truth and understanding.
Sometimes I am so frozen in my ideas and thoughts,
Frozen into icebergs where the polar bears play,
And the seals slip across me into the winter waters.

I know the south, and I love her,
And I love her warmth and her serenity,
And the shaman saguaro cactuses
That lift their spirit to the sky,
Standing like the glaciers,
Like the great trees of the north
In their silence and serenity and perfection.
Maybe one day, Great Spirit,
I will stand like them,
A perfect antenna between your universe and stars
And the moon and the sun,
And the Great Mother Earth beneath.
I love you, Great Spirit,
And I am here to express your love forever. Ho!

Evening Sunset Prayer

Great Spirit, as I see the
Sunset in the western sky,
I think of life on Mother Earth,
And I wonder at the psyche
Of the vast expanse of humanity.
How can we not see that we are alive today,
And that one day we shall surely die?
If we understand that just as the sun sets
In the evening sky and comes up again renewed
In the eastern sky of morning,
So it is with the spirit of each and every one of us.
Why is it that we feel we must accumulate wealth
At the expense of health?
Why is it that human beings, in our magnificence,
In our ability to design and create and believe,
Miss the most important gift you have given us?
We have not learned to make death our ally.
We have not learned to rise and set with the sun.
We have not remembered who we truly are.

As a result we do not honor
The body of our Great Mother Earth,
The body that each of us possesses,
This body that is the temple, the sacred lodge,
Of our spirit, and is our last teacher.
When all else fails,
When we refuse to hear the changes
That we need to make,
When we refuse to learn
What we have come here to learn,
Our body takes over and becomes a last teacher.
Mother Earth has a sensitive body, like our own.
She is in danger now.
She is in danger of dying before her time.
It is up to us to listen to her,
To listen to the earth changes.
Put your ear to the ground,
And listen to the beating of her heart.
What does she tell you in her earthquakes?
What does she tell you in her fires and floods?
Does she wish to hurt us as we have hurt her?
I think not, Great Spirit.

I think she is crying out to be listened to.
If we do not learn the lesson we are here to learn,
She will shrug her shoulders,
And it will all be over for us.
Mother Earth will survive long after we are gone.
So when you look at the sunset,
Thank the Great Spirit for the reminder
That is there, painted across the sky
In oranges and purples and reds and golds.
Remember.
I thank you, Great Spirit,
For all the lessons that you have given us.
And I thank you, Great Spirit,
For the capacity to understand.
I thank you from my heart.
I honor you as I walk with care and truth
On our great Mother Earth.
You have gifted us with your likeness
And the ability to love.
Each and every one of us mirrors
Perfection of spirit back to you in gratitude. Ho!

I Am Full

Someone once said, Great Spirit,
That the only thing to fear is fear itself.
Perhaps there is great wisdom in that comment,
Because I see all around me
The manifestations of fear.
I see unknown diseases running rampant.
Oh Great Spirit, help us to heal our spirits
So that we can heal our health.
Health is the greatest gift you have given us.

As I look at the mountains reflecting the setting sun,
I see the preparation for darkness.
I see the great canyons losing their light,
Moving into a time of hibernation—
The long, dark night of the soul.
But the sun will rise in the morning,
And new light will be brought to those corners
Where shadows lurk and fears abide,
And suddenly, like ghosts in the night,

They are gone, and a new day dawns.
Thank you, Great Spirit, for giving us a new day.
Thank you, for bringing the sun and illuminating
The mountains of endeavor in our lives.
Each of us has a sacred mountain within us,
Great Spirit, and I am climbing,
Ever climbing, toward the top.
Help me on my journey, Great Spirit,
So that one day I can look out across the vast desert
From a new perspective
And see the magnificent mystery of life
As a truly reclaimed dimension of truth.

Great Spirit,
You have sent so many shamans to teach us,
And these shamans stand quiet, in silence,
All around the world,
In the great trees that provide such magnificent shade
From the heat of summer.
The sentinels of saguaro cactus
That guard over the history of the land—
They remember so much that we have forgotten.

Thank you, Great Spirit, for the shamans,
The great stones that create our mountains.
Thank you, Great Spirit, for helping me to climb,
For giving me the will to search out
What is real and true.
You are never ending in your support of me,
And I feel your hand, Great Spirit,
Resting at my back,
Holding me up when I would fall,
Giving me comfort
When I feel the terror of night encroaching.
Help me, Great Spirit, to see now
Across the world from my mountain peak.
Help me to see with new eyes.
Help me to hear your words whispered on the winds.
I know that you send me many allies, Great Spirit.
These allies surround me,
If only I could see them and sense their presence.
I celebrate you, Great Spirit, every day of my life,
And I give thanks for the creation
Of this great schoolhouse called earth.
I thank you for my shaman path,

For the light of the sun,
The dance of the moonlight across my path,
And the stars that lend us their wisdom,
The Pleiades that give us comfort
In the teachings of the ancient ones.
The buffalo roamed here once,
Free and stout and strong.
They have transformed now
Into other places in the universe,
But they have left their memory,
The sound of their hooves
As they would run in herds with the wind.
Great Spirit, forgive us
For not understanding the trail.
Forgive us for our ignorance.
But we will do better, and we are learning,
And we are committed to the path of heart.
Thank you, Great Spirit,
For all that you have given us. Ho!

A Prayer for My Mother and My Father

When two people make the choice
To become parents
Often they know not what lies ahead.
The child who is born to you has chosen you.
I chose you as my parents, and I chose well.
There has been much pain in my life, and much joy.
I realize that I carry a spirit shield
Like a soul from lifetime to lifetime,
And that spirit shield is imprinted with
Every experience throughout my history.
Mother and father, you gave me the blessings
Of your experience.
You marked my trail and held my hand
And taught me the best that you could.
You were there for me in times of need.
You trained me to walk with a foot
In the physical world and a foot in spirit.
I feel your presence always,
Even though you have moved to the other side.

I hear you still in my dreams, and I see your faces,
And I know that the misunderstandings
That we have had over the years
Are understood now because
There is no personality between us.
There is only pure spirit and pure love.
You gave me all that you were,
And I honor you for your efforts
And the pain that you endured on my account,
There is always pain, for children present
A sacred mirror to those who have given them life.
Mirrors are painful to look into.
Often we turn away, not wanting the challenge.
You looked into that mirror,
And you held your gaze strong,
And let me know what was true.
I hope that I heard you.
I hope and pray that I will learn what
I have come here to do
In a way that would make you proud.
I thank you, my mother and my father,
For all that you have given me. Ho!

Prayer for Entering Menopause

Sacred Mother, I pray to you today,
For I am in need of understanding.
I am arriving at the mid-time of my life.
I am going through the gateway of wise blood,
And I need your empowerment, for I am confused.
I have moved through the rites of passage —
Puberty and marriage, child-bearing years—
And now, my society says that I am going to seed.
So now, Great Mother, I am faced with confusion.
There is no one to turn to: My doctors know not.
Many of my sisters do not honor this passage.
I look to your guidance and wisdom, Great Mother,
I hear your voice in the night
When I have fallen into fears
That I have never known before.
I feel the heat of you,
And I hear your voice telling me that this heat
Is my transformation,

That you are making my body ready
For higher consciousness,
That in these coming years, the last half of my life,
I will be moving into my great spiritual time.
I feel your support, and I feel your sadness
And wonderment at my terrors.
I'm afraid that I will not be loved,
That I will not be beautiful,
That those who have cared for me will leave me.
You comfort me in the night.
I can feel your arms around me.
I sense that this is a great gateway, indeed —
That I am a woman at the edge of two worlds
And that I have prepared carefully,
And for a long time for my spirit life,
And I am ready now — I welcome this gateway.
But, Great Mother, stay with me.
Hear me if I begin to falter on my path.
Great Mother, I love you, and I thank you
For helping me to understand my goddess self.
As you have shown me in my visions,
I, too, will walk in beauty the rest of my days. Ho!

A Prayer for Abundance

Money is the trade beads
Of the twentieth century.
Great Spirit, how may I better string
The beads of abundance in my life?
Often I have thought that money was an evil thing,
And I have been afraid to accumulate
Any kind of wealth,
But now I understand, Great Spirit,
That you have given me a great teaching:
That I am worthy of comfort and warmth
In the evening when it is cold,
That I do not have to go without to be a sacred being.
You have taught me well, Great Spirit.
I have worked hard in my life.
I have been afraid to be paid for my efforts,
Because I thought it was wrong.
But I was the one who was wrong, Great Spirit.
I took your gifts and threw them back in your face.
But the gift of abundance is the same

As the gift of a sacred pipe,
Or the energy that abounds in a newborn child.
All the energy of this earth is from you, Great Spirit.
It is your body; it is your blood;
It is the breath of what you are,
The creative force of all that is.
So for me to turn my back on your gifts is an insult.
Abundance is the breath of the Great Spirit.
I thank you, Great Spirit, for helping me understand
That we are indeed all one on this great Mother Earth,
And that as I become abundant,
I help others to become abundant.
If you give to me,
It does not make someone else less fortunate.
Quite to the contrary, Great Spirit, I now see that
It gives those who have less the courage to
Follow their dreams, to manifest in their lives
All that they need.
Thank you, Great Spirit, for the abundance of nature
And all that lives in this universe.
I am filled with gratefulness, Great Spirit,
For all that you have shown me. Ho!

Winter

Taking Stock

Now, in winter, the blossoms and leaves have fallen to the earth. The branches of the trees bend toward the source of their birth. Winter is a time, symbolically, when all returns to what has given life, and the cycles are complete. There has been birth and the fullness of life, and now there is death. The implied lessening of light and the profound shadows of sleep hug the earth.

Winter is a time of hibernation, not only physically but spiritually. It is a time for understanding the great Mother Bear within each of us. Mother Bear is the great dreamer, the hibernator, the one who moves into the silence and the stillness of her own cave to contemplate the Great Spirit and to understand more deeply all that has occurred in the past year. Pray for the Great Spirit to show you the way. For now, as you have reaped the effects of what you have become over the past year, it is a time to choose anew. It is a time to think about the life that you have created. Have you accomplished what you set out to do? Did you miss the mark? Or did you place your arrow well into the target, chosen from the integrity of your own circle of truth?

Winter is a time of gathering what you have accomplished so that you can look toward spring as a time of new beginnings, freshness, new life, and rebirth. Winter is a time for once again pulling back the bow and discovering what the target is in front of you so that when you aim the arrow in the spring, you can aim truly into the central essence of your life, and strike truly at what is needed for your coming year.

During the wintertime, may you experience love, beauty, and peace in your inner cave of hibernation. May you awaken from the long dream of winter into the golden light of all that you have become.

A Prayer for the Winter

Great Spirit, as we move into a time
Of shorter days and longer nights,
Not unlike the winter of our lives,
We experience the coolness of your brilliance.

Star Shield Mother, who empowers my intent,
Great Spirit, give me courage to face my own frailty.
Give me courage to walk on the path of heart.
And if I have failed you,
Help me to understand how I can better
Tear away the veils of ignorance,
And live more fully in the coming year.
Help me, Great Spirit and Mother Star Shield,
To manifest my act of power,
To provide a mirror for my sisters and brothers
Of integrity and impeccability,
As a warrior of the spirit.
Great Spirit, I am yours in my heart and soul.
As I lie down for the long winter to pray

To more deeply understand my true nature,
And the nature of this Great Mother Earth,
My spirit is like a hollow log filled with your light.
May I never lose touch with what is real and true.
May I touch the snows of winter with my fingertips,
And be reminded of the purity of your being.
May I see the reflection of your face
In all of the beings who surround me.
In my long dream, through the long winter night,
May I receive symbols from you
That will deepen my understanding
And help me to go beyond the limits of language
Into the dreamtime.
I await the imprinting of your knowledge
Into my emptiness.
Help me to understand, Great Spirit
All that I have come here to learn in this lifetime.
As I move into the sacred dreamtime of the winter,
I offer my prayers and gratitude and love,
Oh Great Spirit, for my life. Ho!

Prayer in Times of Sadness

Great Spirit, oh Great Sacred Mother,
Oh Grandmother, keeper of the thunder drums,
You bring up in me my passion
And my sense of grief and sadness
For all the imperfections that I see.
I reach out my hands to all people,
That we may share our traditions and our hearts
Across cultural boundaries,
So that our Great Mother Earth may be healed.
There are times when my sadness overcomes me,
And my tears seem for nothing,
And yet I know that with each tear that I shed,
The light of you, Great Spirit, is reflected
Into the universe,
And somehow new beauty is created every day.
There are times, Great Spirit,
When I falter on my path, times when I doubt,
Because of the pain so visible in the world today.
I want so much to heal this pain.

When I move into my own body, Great Spirit,
And I search out the source of my pain,
Again I enter into the emptiness of silence,
And at first a great darkness envelops me,
And I am healed.
In these moments I realize
That darkness truly does define the light,
And that when you reach out into the world
With the voice of truth,
Healing occurs and even darkness is illumined.
I ask you, Great Spirit, to listen to our voices,
And take the energy for your healing process.
Let our words, our prayers, and the voices of our drums
Bring light into the world,
So that renewed harmony and balance
Can live once again.
When I am overcome with sadness
At what this world has become as a result of us,
I am also filled with joy,
Because I know that somehow in
The great design of creation, everything is perfect,
And that lessons need to be learned,

Sometimes in the most difficult of ways.
I know deep in my heart, Great Spirit,
That I have chosen my vision,
That I have chosen my relationships,
That I have indeed chosen my circumstances in life.
There is no question, Great Sacred Mother,
That through pain and confusion and difficulty,
Growth occurs.
Out of the mud at the bottom of a reflection pond
Grows the magnificent lotus blossom
In a state of perfection.
Great Mother Earth, you will rise out of the ashes
Like a phoenix at dawn, and be healed.
You are the source of all power,
And we honor you, Great Mother Earth,
With our prayers, with the heartbeat of creation,
Through the voice of our drums.
Thank you, Great Spirit,
Thank you, Great Mother,
For being with us always. Ho!

Prayer to Ask for Help

Blessed beings of the lower world,
Come to me and show your sacred four directions.
Spirit beings who protect and empower me,
See my humbleness,
And hear the sound of my beating heart.
Sacred Mother and Father Sky,
Be with me now.

When I am alone and afraid,
I search the sky
For a sign from you, Great Spirit.
I place my hands on you,
Mother Earth, and feel the beating
Of your abundant heart.
Then why do I feel this pain,
When your beauty is all around me?

Sometimes I cannot see,
And it is now that I seek pure vision.

Forgive me, Great Spirit, for my ignorance.
For you have shared the radiant
Miracle of life with me.
I feel the wind from the north,
And I remember Spirit.
I remember Trickster Coyote in the east
As he nips at my heels and tests my sacred intent.
Help me, Great Spirit, for I need you now.
I need to remember who I am
And see your reflection in the red sky at dawn.
I see ahead of me your footsteps in
The sands of time,
And I follow you with love
And a humble heart.

I pray for your guidance,
And I will listen now for your words inside me,
Like the gentle wind.
Let there be silence.
Let there be peace in my soul
And in the souls of all living things. Ho!

A Prayer for Balance

Oh Great Mother, as I look out
Across the desert, green from rain,
And see the mountains in the distance,
I ask that you guide me along my path of heart.
I ask that you help me to understand
My powers of creativity.
As the clouds above me
Cast shadows on the desert floor,
I know that I have often lost my way,
And when the shadow aspects of myself
Diminish my life, I become afraid.
Oh Great Mother, take my hand.
Help me to see the trail,
So that I may find my way home.
Sometimes I think I will be bereft of balance forever,
That there is no one to help me.
But as I look at the great mountains in the distance,
As their silhouette is etched against the sky
With such clarity,

I know that somewhere in my heart
I have known such clarity before,
And that you are there for me.
It is only I who sometimes refuse to see you.
I will open my eyes now, and I will see your face,
Just as the sunlight bursting through the clouds
Illuminates the flowers all around me.
I will begin to shine as they do.
I am flowering for you, Great Mother.
I am lending my beauty to the universe
For a short time, and I realize that this life is a process
Of seed and stalk, growth and flowering, then death.
But death is only a rebirth back into spirit,
A rebirth back into life.
And you may call me anytime, Great Spirit,
Back into your arms.
So I am here for you, Great Mother, Great Spirit.
I am like a hollow log with your love and energy
Flowing through me forever.
Help me to walk in beauty and power
All the days of my life. Ho!

Masks of the Four Directions

Great Spirit, powers of the four directions,
My medicine, my allies, my ancestors,
And all those who love me,
Thank you for being with me today.

Great Spirit, I hold up my shaman face of the south.
In trust and innocence, I give this face to the world.
It is the child within me who sees through this mask,
Who sees into the world with humbleness and stillness.
Inside I am still the bright-eyed child,
Looking out at the world with hope and joy.
Great Spirit, may you tend to me on my path.

Oh great Powers of the West,
Powers of the sacred dream, death and rebirth,
Of transformation, see my shaman face,
That part of me that dares to dream,
That dares to move out into the world.

My eyes look through the eyes of this shaman face,
The eyes of my adolescent self,
That part of me that is so full of emotions,
That part of me that needs to understand
The dimensions of death and life
And the never-ending circle of creation.

Oh great, formidable Powers of the North,
Home of White Buffalo Woman,
Who brought the sacred pipe to her people,
Powers of the North, strength and wisdom, spirit,
I hold up my shaman face with pride.
I look through the eyes of my adult self,
And I see the world with courage and strength.
I stand in my power self, holding my shaman face
For all the world to see, and I am not afraid.

Powers of the East, with your illumination
And your golden sun that shines so high in the sky,
Help me to know the other faces of my inner circle.
Help me to bring light
Into those dark corners of my being,

So that I may understand even the dark side of myself,
That I may accept my frailties as well as my strengths.
Place of illumination, place of the sacred clown,
Help me to test the existing institutions in my life,
With understanding and knowledge.
Place of illumination, my shaman face of power,
You help me understand what is real and what is true.
Hear my voice
As I speak through my shaman face of the East,
And know that I stand in the place of self,
In the center of my sacred wheel.

Great Spirit, I have my four shaman faces around me,
And I know that I can wear one or another
As is appropriate in my life.
Give me the vision to move into my life with power.
Give me the wisdom to know what is right and true.
As I see light in the world,
I reflect that light with the courage of my being.
Great Spirit, I am yours to do your will,
To live in the light forevermore. Ho!

Prayer for Healing

I am a wise one.
I come from the faraway,
And I can lead you there.
I walk with the winds.
I am an important one.
I cling to the life of the spirit.
I am a false face healer.
I walk with the power of the sun
Around the mysteries of life.
I heal the mind and the heart.
I am an important one.
I am a being of sacred words.
I unravel the mysteries of your pain
So that you may find courage.
May you learn to follow the sacred ways.
I am of the light and the holy ones.
I walk in the land of spirit,
And I walk on the earth.
I honor all that is sacred. Ho!

A Prayer for the Night

I pray to you, Goddess Mother,
Keeper of all living things,
I pray to you for the night,
For the magnificent shroud of shadows
That overcomes us
As the sun disappears on the western horizon.
Night, you give me sleep,
You give me rest,
And you give me peace when all is well.

Great Goddess Mother,
I feel your arms around me,
Comforting me.
I feel your hand at my back,
Caressing me and keeping
The night shadows of worry
From tormenting me.
When I sleep, there are times when
Some strange energy envelops me,

And I feel the pains of everyday life as if they were
Magnified in the reflection of a great pond,
In numbers beyond counting.
I call these the terrors of the night.

When I am so tired that I seem to have no resistance,
Great Goddess Mother, protect me from all harm,
And allow me to slumber in peace,
For you are the keeper of the night,
And I lend my gratitude
For the fullness of my heart
To your queenly observance and vigilance,
For surely you are there,
As surely as I breathe.
I can feel the cloaks of your gown,
Keeping me warm and holding
The power that keeps me safe.
Thank you for allowing me to heal in peace,
In the tranquillity of the night. Ho!

Prayer for the Wisdom of the Elders

Great Elder Women, Great Wise Men,
Elders who encircle us in the physical dimension,
This earthly walk,
Thank you for your courage and your holy blessings.
As I look out at the desert,
Magnificent in its purple and gold shadows
Of the early morning,
The golden light recalls in my memory
The power and the blessings that the elders
Bestow on us all.
I thank you for your courage to live,
And to remain on this earthly plane.
With all that you see, with all that you hear,
You give us so much in your prayers,
In your understanding,
Sharing your power every step of the way.
As I look across the sand, I see the footsteps of
Those who have walked before us,

And I know the courage and the commitment
That it takes to stay on the path of heart.
Great Elder Beings who have given so much,
This is a prayer of thanksgiving for who you are,
For so many of you are maligned for your
Beauty and your silence.
I honor your presence.
Just your existence and radiance illuminate our path
And bring us closer to Great Spirit
And to the magnificence that you are.
Without you, our trail would be arduous
Beyond imagination.
So few realize how you mark our trail,
Because what you do is done in silence.
Your gifts are unnamed and anonymous.
Thank you for your blessings.
Thank you for being there when we are so weak,
But once you were weak, and you understand.
And if you were to ask for anything,
It would be for our commitment to the goodness
And the beauty and the love
That we are made of, as you are. Ho!

A Prayer for Life and Death

When I think of our sojourn
On this earthly plane,
I think of you, Great Spirit,
As you enter my world
Daily in the morning light,
Bringing life to the flowers
And all that lives.

When I think of your passing,
My dear friend,
I think of your light
As it illuminated my spirit
All the days of your life.

And when you left me and went on
Into the arms of the Great Spirit,
I cried in my grief,
Forgetting that
You had simply moved

From my earthly vision.
I am in pain because I miss you so.
I miss being able to reach out and touch you.

And yet, when I close my eyes,
You are inside of me,
You are forever within me,
And as I look at the setting sun,
I am reminded
Of the brilliance of your walk on this earth,
And how you illumined
Those around you.
You were a prime mover for me.
You made me circle my truth
And stand in my center,
And I am grateful always for how
You stood strong with me.

I honor you always,
And I hope that you felt
That respect and joy in your lifetime—
How you filled me

With peace and strength.
Surely, without you,
I could not have walked
My path of wisdom.
Because of your passing to the other side,
I realize more than ever
That we are all one.
And because of your oneness with all that is,
I even more fully sense
My oneness on this earth walk.

When I smell the beautiful roses,
I know that you live
Within that scent.
When I feel the gentle rains
Coming from the clouds,
I know it is the essence of your spirit
I feel on my skin.
When the wind blows
And I feel it caressing my cheek
Like fine silk,
I know that it is you.

Thank you, Great Spirit,
For this process of life and death.
It ennobles us beyond
Our distinction as human beings.
We become gods;
We become you.
And I walk in beauty
All the days of my life,
Knowing that you are within me. Ho!

Gratitude
and
World Peace

Opening the Heart

*I*n a sense, all prayers are prayers of gratitude, for as you open your heart, even in the midst of your pain and sadness, or your joy and wonder, you cannot help but find yourself grateful for the multitude of small blessings that exist through all the seasons of your life.

Out of your gratitude flows the natural impulse to praise Great Spirit and Mother Earth for the magnificence that surrounds you. There is a difference between gratitude and gratefulness. In gratitude, you sit in stillness within the center of your being, hailing the bliss and the love that you have for creation. Gratitude provides an opening of the heart that brings in your God, while gratefulness leads to action. Gratefulness is a moving out toward the world, toward all people and all living things, with open arms and an open heart.

It seems so difficult for human beings to be grateful for long. We look at the stars, magnificent in the night sky. We observe the sun in its brilliance, and we forget to be grateful for what is simply all around us—the act of God, the act of life. We walk on Mother Earth. We take part in her beauty every time we open our eyes. Even in the most difficult of situations, there is always a magnificent sky above us. Why is it that we forget who we are? For truly we are the reflections of our maker. If only we open our hearts with gratefulness, the clouds that obscure the face of God will lift, and the Great Spirit will shine upon us.

There are times when I am overcome with grief for our great Mother Earth, and I wonder what one person can possibly do. Then I remember that the earth is a schoolhouse, and we have come here to move along that great path of enlightenment and self-realization. World peace can only come when we open our hearts and our arms to all cultures, to all forms of life. I have always celebrated the differences in ways of seeing reality, because these differences are what make life so interesting.

In the name of God, in the name of the Great Spirit, I celebrate all of life. I hope that you will join with me in prayer, and let our prayers be for the radiance of the Great Spirit within us to illumine the dark places within our souls that are sad and bereft of balance. With open and grateful hearts, let us pray for world peace, for hope upon this land. Let us pray for the goodness that all human beings truly are. May you walk in beauty all the days of your life.

A Prayer of Gratitude

Great Spirit, Mother Earth,
Powers of the four directions,
My medicine, my power animal, my ancestors,
And all those who love me,
This is a prayer of gratitude,
For the life force that gives me form
And animation in this lifetime.
Great Sacred Mother,
You have protected me all the days of my life.
I have felt your hand in the center of my back,
Supporting me in moments of fear and confusion.
Great Father Sun,
I have felt your warmth in my heart,
When I have been in grief and pain,
When I have misunderstood the actions of others.
I have felt your healing magnificence,
Oh Great Spirit, in my shaman center.
There are moments when I lose my will
And the courage to go on.

There are times, Great Spirit,
When I look in ponds of water,
And for a moment,
I think that I have seen the reflection
Of your beautiful face instead of my own.
In those moments,
Through the trials of separation and duality
That all of us have experienced,
I realize that, in fact, we are all one,
That you bless us,
And that you guide our feet on the path of life,
Every step we take,
If only we give ourselves the chance to listen.
I give thanks to the great winds, my allies,
The winds of the four directions,
That guide me down my path toward enlightenment.

I have found in these past years
That it doesn't matter who speaks the truth,
As long as the truth is spoken,
That none of us owns the truth.

Even if an idea comes into my head,
I know that that idea is from you, Great Spirit,
And from you, Mother Earth,
And that through the beauty of existence,
You are teaching us with the mirrors of your perfection.
Great Spirit, Great Sacred Mother,
I feel your blessings in my body.
In my moon, I feel
The cleansing strength of your power.
And when I begin to lose my way,
If I remember to listen to my heart and open my eyes
To the birds, the great winged ones, who fly above me,
If I let myself smell the fragrance of all that lives,
I know that you are within me,
And that I am within you.
Great Spirit, oh Sacred Mother,
I honor you, and I give thanks
From my heart to yours,
For my life and for my path,
And for the truth that we all share. Ho!

A Thanksgiving Prayer

Great Spirit, Mother Earth,
Powers of the four directions, my ancestors,
And all those who love me, hear me now.
This is a prayer of thanksgiving for the miracle of life.
When I awake in the morning, Great Spirit,
And I take a breath of morning air,
I look toward the sky, searching the morning light
For your face,
And when I find it, a radiance comes to me,
So beautiful and so blissful
That I cannot put words to the gratefulness
That is in my heart.
There is much pain and confusion in this world.
And oftentimes I lose my way,
And I know not what to do.
Then I sit in silence, and I listen
To the high north wind in the pine trees,
And you sing to me.
I open my eyes and I look at the flowers

And the miracle of beauty that they are.
Again I see your face,
And I wonder at my ignorance.
So days go by, and I follow my path of heart,
And I pray to you, Great Spirit,
Grateful and strong from your grace.
The four-leggeds and the winged ones
Bring joy to my life,
And I thank you for their presence all around me.
Their purity of being reminds me of you,
And I know that they are mirrors,
Shiny and brilliant with your reflection.
I know that much gives away so that I may live.
The sacred give-away I receive and return,
Ever grateful for your flowing power within me.
Without you, I could not see the beauty
That you have given us.
I feel the sun on my face, and I know your warmth,
And I know that somehow everything is perfect.
I give thanks as I walk my path of beauty.
For you I live all the days of my life. Ho!

A Prayer of Thanks for the Animals

When I need the greatest solace,
I go to the animals for support.
All animals are sacred.
They live in a state of purity.
A donkey cannot be other than a donkey.
A winged one cannot be other than a bird.
And some might say that a human
Cannot be other than a human.
But, to me, that is not so.
We humans have a kind of choice in our lives
That animals do not have,
And because of that,
Their kind of ignorance is bliss.
They have a wisdom in their eyes,
If we only sit within the circle of our own truth
And listen from our hearts.
We owe an extraordinary debt to the animals.
We use and we eat without an understanding
Of the sacred give-away.

This is a prayer, Great Spirit, of gratitude.
This is a prayer of honoring for all the animals —
The winged ones and the four-leggeds
Who walk this earth.
They give away so often so that we may live,
And we, in our kind of ignorance,
Do not understand what we do.
Oh magical and sacred horses,
Whose hoof beats can be heard in the night,
Unicorns, that run through our dreams
And take us away into other dimensions
Of higher consciousness,
Horses, who give us their backs,
So that we may ride them,
They give over their will to ours,
And yet so often we misuse our power.
Great Mother Eagle, circling high in the skies above,
Floating on the air drafts of pure perfection,
Eagles, feathers glistening in the sun,
Your screams echo through the mountain canyons,
Filling me with awe and inspiration.
South Ones, whose noses are closest to the ground,

Field Mouse, whose life is so tender and sweet,
You live close to Mother Earth,
One of her special ones, tiny, darting, waiting,
Yours is the art of listening.
If only we could listen as well
In the art of shamanism.
Many speak about what they know.
They will tell you endlessly about their powers,
And you know, instantly, their flaw.
They don't know how to listen like the field mouse.
Sacred cats, you test your claws
And move with stealth and cunning
Through the jungles and the mountains and
The plains of the world, you are a predator.
You know how to survive.
You are strong and sleek.
You are a warrior beyond compare.
Great dreaming bear of the west,
You who gather knowledge and
Wisdom throughout the year,
And hibernate in the long winter,
Holding close what you have learned,

Practicing your art of silence and slumber,
But when you awaken, you are a power
To be reckoned with.
Your eyesight may be limited,
But the vision from your power center
Is beyond measure,
And your wisdom lives in the sacred dreamtime.
And dogs, sacred puppies,
You are in this world to absorb our pain and our grief.
May you be thanked properly by those who keep you.
May you be loved and trusted
For the magnificent beings that you are.
This is a prayer for all of the four-leggeds
And the winged ones.
May we not misuse our power against you.
May we live in balance
In all the four directions of the earth of the spirit,
To support you and join you
In your pure reality. Ho!

Morning Light Awakens

As the morning light walks in the land,
I think of you, Great Spirit,
Of the way you have illumined
The dark corners of my soul.
Morning light,
As you awaken the plants
And glisten off the pine needles
Of these great trees,
I hear you coming, Great Spirit.
The birds sing their welcome
And speak of your presence among us.
In a blaze of splendor and golden light,
You warm our lives.
As the forest comes to life,
I, too, am quickened, Great Spirit.
I see you in the morning light,
And my soul is filled with your beauty.
My heart is full. Ho!

A Prayer for Peace

Oh Great Spirit,
The sacred blanket of life
Keeps me warm when I am cold.
In these days of transition,
I take the sacred blankets
That you have given us,
And I remember how
You taught us to pray.

I take the black threads of the west,
And I tie them with
The golden threads of the east,
As I offer a prayer for
Illumination of my spirit.
I ask, as I tie the knot,
For harmony between east and west,
For the veils of ignorance
To be torn away forever
Between all people.

I remember, Great Spirit,
Sacred Mystery,
When you guided my fingers
To the white threads of the north —
The threads of spirit and wisdom.
You showed me how to tie them
With the red fibers of the south —
The threads of substance.

I pray over the sacred ties
Of this great blanket,
And I ask for peace
From the innocent and trusting child
That is my soul.

I wrap my humble body
With your proud blanket
Of peace and harmony,
Forever. Ho!

Epilogue:
Prayer Can Change the World

You have prayed through the four seasons of the soul, through the cycles of your life. You have dreamed, and you have accomplished, and you have grieved. The wisdom of your prayers is upon you. Have you succeeded? Are you joyous about the work of art that you have created called your life? Truly, you are a painter on a giant canvas of miraculous life force. There is nothing in my way of knowledge that is more magical than a human being who has become self-realized, who has become enlightened. When we are enlightened, we assume a great responsibility to the universe of people who inhabit Mother Earth.

Long ago, I was sitting at the foot of the Annapurna Himal, on the border of Tibet in Nepal with my teachers, Agnes Whistling Elk, Ruby Plenty Chiefs, and Ani, a Nepalese hill woman who is a member of the Sisterhood of the Shields. There was a river coursing down from the Himalayas, rushing by us down into the rolling plains of Nepal. We were having tea, and I took a spoonful of sugar and dumped it in the river coursing by. In an instant, the sugar disappeared. I looked at my teachers tearfully, and I said, "That is what I feel about the dedication of my life to our work, to healing the earth and her people. I feel that my work is lost in a torrent of ignorance. How can I—how can anyone—ever make a difference?"

As Agnes and Ruby so often do when I take myself too seriously, they pulled my consciousness around and made me laugh. Then Agnes turned her magnificent eyes to search my face. Finally, she reached out her hand and covered my palm with hers. "My daughter," she said, "you have only one responsibility in this lifetime, and that is to enlighten yourself. You cannot take the responsibility for anyone else. And remember, you cannot truly heal or help another person; you can only provide, at the best of times, an environment within which others can heal and find themselves. And that is all that you or anyone can do."

"Pray," Ruby Plenty Chiefs said. "Prayer can change the world. Your light will affect all of those around you and give them the strength and the inspiration to go on and celebrate the magnificence of what they are."

I dried my tears and held Agnes's hand. I watched her beautiful face etched so deeply by time and experience. "For me," I finally said, "prayer is the expression of innocence. It is our radiant bridge to Great Spirit. Through the grateful heart in innocence, all things are possible."

Enter a Cosmology of Mystery, Magic, and Power With Lynn Andrews

For the last ten years, I have been describing my learning and my path. It has been a joy to do this. In continuing my journey, I would be grateful if you would share your insights with me.

In addition, you are invited to join me at my June retreat in the high Mojave desert for four days of ceremony, sacred community, meditation, and healing. Please call or write for scheduled dates and detailed information. In addition, expanded in-depth training is available at the Lynn Andrews Center for Arts and Training, beginning each February. Also available are over twenty audio tapes, beautifully produced and digitally recorded, including guided meditations and a very special selection of teachings, personal reflections, and sacred music.

Please send me your name and address so I can share any new information with you:

Lynn Andrews
2934 ½ Beverly Glen Circle
Box 378
Los Angeles, CA 90077
I (800) 726-0082